LIVING WITH EPILEPSY

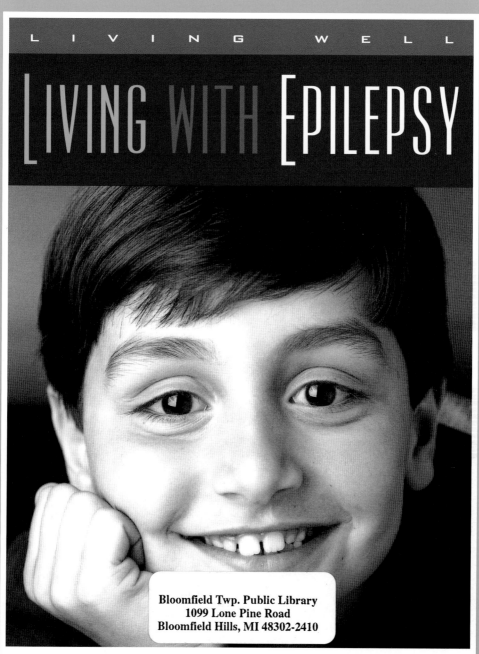

by Shirley Wimbish Gray

THE CHILD'S WORLD®
CHANHASSEN, MINNESOTA

The publisher wishes to sincerely thank Patricia M. Barry, R.N., C.S., P.N.P., for her help in preparing this book for publication.

Published in the United States of America by the Child's World®
P.O. Box 326, Chanhassen, MN 55317-0326
800-599-READ
www.childsworld.com

Photo Credits: Cover: Nicole Katano/Brand X Pictures/Corbis, Custom Medical Stock Photo, Inc. (inset); Al Behrman/Associated Press: 20; Lionel Cironneau/Associated Press: 5; White House/Associated Press: 19; Corbis: 18 (top); Andrea Appiani/Corbis: 18 (bottom); Nicole Katano/Brand X Pictures/Corbis: 1; Roger Ressmeyer/Corbis: 15, 29; Phil Schermeister/Corbis: 25 (bottom); Custom Medical Stock Photo, Inc.: 7, 9, 14; Adam Jones/Dembinsky Photo Associates: 23; Dan Dempster/Dembinsky Photo Associates: 25 (top); FPG/GettyImages: 12; The Image Bank/GettyImages: 22; Stone/GettyImages: 16, 17, 21, 26, 27; Tom Carter/PhotoEdit: 8; Tom McCarthy/PhotoEdit: 6; Michael Newman/PhotoEdit: 11; Eric R. Berndt/Unicorn Stock Photos: 13 (bottom); Tom McCarthy/Unicorn Stock Photos: 13 (top)

The Child's World®: Mary Berendes, Publishing Director

Editorial Directions, Inc.: E. Russell Primm, Editor; Alice Flanagan, Photo Researcher; Linda S. Koutris, Photo Selector; The Design Lab, Designer and Page Production; Red Line Editorial, Fact Researcher; Irene Keller, Copy Editor; Tim Griffin/IndexServ, Indexer; Donna Frassetto, Proofreader

Library of Congress Cataloging-in-Publication Data
Gray, Shirley W.
  Living with epilepsy / by Shirley Wimbish Gray.
      v. cm.— (Living Well series)
Includes index.
Contents: Do you know someone who has epilepsy?—What is epilepsy?—What's a seizure like?—What can we do about epilepsy?—Who gets epilepsy?—Will we ever cure epilepsy?
  ISBN 1-56766-103-3
  1. Epilepsy—Juvenile literature. [1. Epilepsy. 2. Diseases.] I. Title. II. Series.
  RC372.2 .G73 2002
  618.92'853—dc21   2002002869

TABLE OF CONTENTS

CHAPTER ONE

Do You Know Someone Who Has Epilepsy?

Marion Clignet was a teenager when she had her first **seizure.** She did not know what happened. Later, the doctors told her she had epilepsy (EP-uh-lep-see).

Marion soon found out that she was not allowed to have a driver's license because she might have another seizure while she was driving. But how could she get to work? She did not want other people to drive her everywhere. So she started riding her bike.

Marion learned that medicine could control her seizures. She also learned how to ride her bike fast. She started entering bike races. She got faster and began winning races. Then, in 1996, she won a silver medal in the Summer Olympic Games!

Maybe you know somebody like Marion who has epilepsy. Or maybe you have it yourself. In 1995, almost 300,000 children aged 14 and under had epilepsy. Children who have epilepsy learn how to live with it. That is what Marion did. You can help by learning about epilepsy, too.

Marion Clignet is an Olympic silver-medal winner.

CHAPTER TWO

WHAT IS EPILEPSY?

The word *epilepsy* is a Greek word meaning to "to hold or seize." Children who have epilepsy have seizures. The Greeks thought that seizures "took hold" of the body. People may have seizures when something goes wrong in their brain.

The brain works with electricity, sort of like a lamp does. In a house, electrical current travels over a wire to the lamp. The electricity makes the lamp light up. In the body, brain cells send electrical signals through the nerves. These signals make our muscles move.

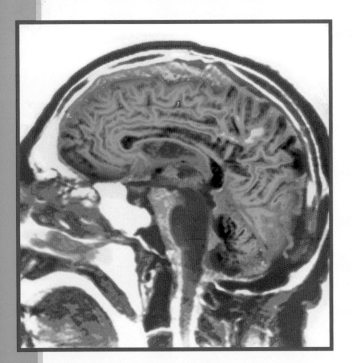

A color-enhanced brain scan

Sometimes too many brain cells send signals at the same time, and this causes an overload. The muscles do not know what to do. They might tighten up like a fist. Then they might relax. This could happen over and over, and very quickly. This is called a seizure.

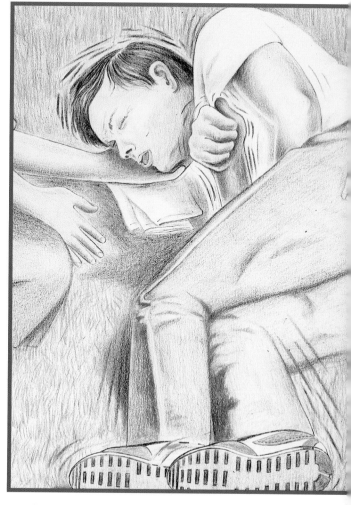

This boy is having a seizure, but is in a safe position on the floor with a friend helping him.

Sometimes the muscles freeze. They do not move at all. This is also a seizure. A child having a seizure may have no control over the muscles. A seizure stops when the cells stop sending the wrong signals. Seizures are scary to look at, but they do not hurt.

Head injuries, such as those received in car accidents, can cause seizures.

Having just one seizure does not mean that a child has epilepsy.

Lots of things can trigger one. Hurting the head in a car wreck could

cause a seizure, for example. Having a high fever could also cause one.

About half of the children who have a seizure never have another one.

We say a person has epilepsy when that person has two or more

seizures. Doctors do not know why this happens. One child may have

a seizure every day. Another child may have one every few months.

If a child has a seizure, the doctor will do some tests. Some of these tests study the brain. They measure the signals sent by the brain cells. Other tests check the blood. These blood tests help the doctor find out if the child needs medicine to stop the seizures.

There are many types of epilepsy. Some types only affect children. Some may be linked to **genes.** Other kinds of epilepsy are linked to other health problems. Doctors still have a lot to learn about epilepsy.

A doctor reviews the brain waves of an epilepsy patient.

CHAPTER THREE

WHAT'S IT LIKE TO HAVE EPILEPSY?

Seizures are not all alike. There are two main types. The most common type is called a generalized seizure. This kind of seizure starts all at once throughout the brain. A child having a generalized seizure may fall and black out. Sometimes people throw up or lose control of their **bladder.** Their muscles often twitch and jerk.

A generalized seizure usually lasts for several minutes. Children do not remember having this type of seizure. They feel tired and sleepy when it is over.

The second kind of seizure is a partial, or focal, seizure. It involves a small part of the brain and may cause a child to just stop and stare. A teacher may think the child is daydreaming. The muscles seem to freeze. Children having a partial seizure may not know where they are.

After a seizure, people with epilepsy are often tired and sleepy.

Usually, a person having a seizure does not need first aid. Seizures end by themselves. People used to think that children could swallow their tongue during seizures, but this is not true.

Sometimes people have a funny taste in their mouth right before

Wearing proper safety equipment for a bike ride is always a good idea.

a seizure occurs, or they smell something strange. Others say they have a weird feeling. This taste or feeling or strange smell is called an aura. But most of the time there is no warning at all.

People who have epilepsy must be careful. They do not know where they will be when they have a seizure. Suppose a friend had a seizure while riding a bike. Chances are your friend would be hurt, and the bike would be wrecked.

Bright flashing lights can sometimes trigger a seizure. So your friend might have one while playing a video game or watching TV.

Other things can trigger seizures, too. Feeling stressed and not getting enough sleep can also bring them on. A teenager might be worried about a test and stay up late studying. The worry and the lack of sleep could trigger a seizure.

The flashing lights of a video game or the stress of studying can trigger a seizure.

CHAPTER FOUR

WHAT CAN WE DO ABOUT EPILEPSY?

The good news is that most seizures can be controlled with medicine.

Today, people who have epilepsy can drive cars and hold jobs. They

can do most of the activities they want to do.

For some people, the medicine does not work, though. These

people may decide to have brain **surgery.**

Doctors can sometimes remove

or repair the part of the

brain that sends the mixed-

up signals.

The **vagus nerve**

stimulator (VNS) is another

type of treatment. The VNS uses a

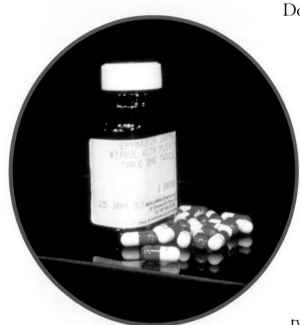

Medicine can control most seizures.

battery that is a little larger than a quarter. The doctor puts the battery

in the patient's chest wall, under the skin. The battery sends electrical

signals to the brain through the vagus nerve, a nerve in the neck. The

vagus nerve is one of the twelve cranial nerves in the human body; it is

like a computer system for the brain. The signal from the VNS can

help stop or prevent seizures.

Some children eat a special diet that helps prevent seizures. It is

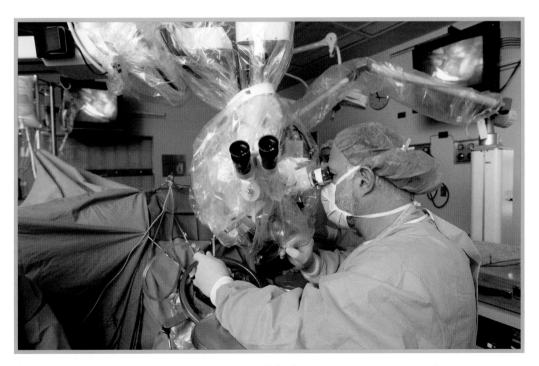

Surgery to remove or repair a part of the brain can sometimes stop seizures.

A diet high in fat and low in carbohydrates is another way to help control seizures.

high in fat and low in carbohydrates. Children can eat cheese and drink cream on this diet. But they cannot have pasta noodles or bread.

This diet is called the ketogenic diet. It produces a change called ketosis in the body's chemistry. Children on this diet must have their blood checked often. Their doctors have to make sure everything is okay. Most children think the diet is not too bad if it helps control their seizures.

Friends can make everyday activities a little safer for those with epilepsy.

Even with these various treatments, seizures may still happen.

Some people must change their lives because of seizures. Everyday

activities could be dangerous for them. What if a person had a

seizure while driving a car? What if a seizure happened while the

person was crossing a busy street or taking a bath?

CHAPTER FIVE

WHO GETS EPILEPSY?

Julius Caesar ruled ancient Rome. Socrates was a teacher during the time of the Greeks. Napoléon was a famous general. Vincent van Gogh's paintings hang in museums around the world today. Each of these people lived hundreds of years ago. They were smart and brave and creative. Each of them had epilepsy.

In 1988, Florence Griffith Joyner won

Julius Caesar (above) and Napoléon (below) both had epilepsy.

three gold medals in the Olympic Games. She set several world records for running fast. Most people called her FloJo. Few people knew that FloJo had epilepsy.

Lots of people know who Danny Glover is. You may have seen him in a movie. Did you know that he also has epilepsy? You

WITH DISABILITIES ACT: OPPORTUNITIES

One day when Tony Coelho was in high school his pickup truck flipped over. He hit his head hard. Later, he started having seizures, and he developed epilepsy.

Tony's life changed. He lost his driver's license and could not get a job. Some people decided he could not do things just because he had epilepsy.

Tony then got into politics. He promised to make life easier for people who had epilepsy and other disabilities. In 1990, Tony and others in Congress passed the Americans with Disabilities Act. Now it is against the law to keep someone from getting a job because of a disability.

Florence Griffith Joyner won three gold medals in the Olympics.

cannot look at someone and know from the outside that they have epilepsy. Anyone can develop epilepsy, even doctors.

Some diseases occur more in one group of people than in another. For example, people who are overweight may develop diabetes. Also, African-American children develop asthma more often than other children do. This is not true of epilepsy, however.

Epilepsy can develop in any kind of person. Children around the world develop it. It occurs in boys and girls, men and women. No one group of people develops it more often than another.

Most seizures occur in children younger than 15

Epilepsy develops in people of all races and ethnic backgrounds.

years old. They are also common in adults older than 65.

Epilepsy is not contagious like colds or flus. It cannot be

Epilepsy is most common in the young and the old.

passed from one person to another. Cerebral palsy and autism

also involve the brain. Many children who have these conditions

also have epilepsy. No one knows why one brain has seizures and

another does not.

CHAPTER SIX

WILL WE EVER CURE EPILEPSY?

People have known about epilepsy for thousands of years, and it has

been called by many different names. Some people called it "the

sacred disease." They thought the ancient gods gave it to humans.

Other people called epilepsy "the falling sickness," because people

often fell when they had a seizure. It was also called a "disease of the

Moon." People thought

the seizures came and

went like the phases of

the Moon.

People also did

things to keep from

"catching" epilepsy.

Long ago people believed the epilepsy came and went like the phases of the Moon.

People were taught to spit if they saw someone who had epilepsy.

That way they could spit out the disease. Others used plants to

help treat the seizures.

Doctors today know more about epilepsy than doctors knew

hundreds of years ago. But they still have lots of unanswered

questions. For example, researchers wonder why brain cells send

too many electrical signals. How do seizures develop? How do

seizures affect the brain? Are genes involved?

Scientists are searching for clues so that they can answer these

questions. The answers might help them find a cure. For example,

some types of epilepsy may run in families. Maybe a grandmother,

an uncle, and a child all had epilepsy.

Doctors want to talk to these family members. They might ask

for samples of blood. Then they could search for a gene that might

Scientists are researching families where a number of members all have epilepsy.

be a clue to epilepsy. Genes

help decide a person's

features, such as hair and

eye color, and decide what

illnesses the person develops.

Doctors and researchers study brain waves to try to understand epilepsy better.

Scientists and doctors need help in their search for more clues.

Sometimes they ask people with epilepsy to take part in clinical trials. These are studies that test new ways to treat the body. Children can be included in clinical trials. Then they become part of the research team.

You can help, too. Do you know someone who has epilepsy?

Researchers study kids with epilepsy to understand it better and to find new treatments.

If so, be a good friend. If your friend has a seizure, do not run away. Maybe you can keep your friend from getting hurt during the seizure. Explain what is happening to anyone who does not understand. Having epilepsy is hard for a child. Having a good friend makes it easier.

Of course, children with epilepsy must try to protect themselves. There is always a chance they could get hurt during their seizures. But they can still have fun. Here are some ideas of how you and your friend with epilepsy can do fun things together.

Wear a helmet, kneepads, and elbow pads when you go bike-riding.

If you have seizures, do not go swimming at all.

Stand back from the curb when you are waiting to cross the street.

During a slumber party, sleep in sleeping bags on the floor instead of bunk beds.

Glossary

bladder (BLAD-uhr) The bladder is the organ in the body where urine is stored.

genes (JEENS) Genes are the part of a cell that decide which features of the parent a child will inherit.

seizure (SEE-zhur) A seizure is a sudden attack of illness, or a spasm.

surgery (SUR-jer-ee) Surgery is a medical treatment in which the body is cut open to remove or repair something.

vagus nerve (VA-guhss NURV) The vagus nerve is one of the carnial nerves in the brain.

Questions and Answers about Epilepsy

What is epilepsy? Epilepsy is a medical condition that causes people to have seizures. It involves the central nervous system of the body. That includes the brain and the nerves. A person who has two or more seizures is said to have epilepsy.

Who gets epilepsy? Anybody can develop epilepsy at any age. Children and adults over the age of 65 have the most seizures.

What causes epilepsy? Some people develop epilepsy after they have a high fever. Others develop epilepsy after a car wreck. Most of the time, people develop it for no apparent reason.

How is epilepsy treated? Medication helps prevent most seizures. Sometimes the medicine cannot control them. Then a person may decide to have brain surgery or vagus nerve stimulator therapy. Some children eat a special diet that helps prevent seizures.

Can I catch epilepsy? No, you cannot catch epilepsy from someone else.

Are all seizures the same? No, there are different types of seizures. Generalized seizures and partial, or focal, seizures are the two most common kinds.

Do seizures hurt? No, they don't. They look scary, but they do not hurt. In fact, the person having the seizure may not even remember what happened after it ends.

Helping a Friend
Who Has Epilepsy

▸ During a seizure, move your friend to a soft, flat area if possible. Grass is better than concrete. Carpet is better than hardwood floors.

▸ Do not put anything into your friend's mouth during a seizure.

▸ Turn your friend to the side if the seizure is a convulsion. This prevents choking if the person throws up.

▸ Do not try to stop your friend's movements. The seizure will stop by itself.

▸ Stay with your friend until the seizure is over. Remember, most people are tired and dazed after a seizure.

▸ When the seizure is over, tell an adult what happened.

Did You Know?

▸ The Bible tells stories about people who had epilepsy.

▸ Saint Valentine is the patron saint of people who have epilepsy.

▸ More than 2 million people have epilepsy—1 person out of every 100.

▸ Humans are not the only living creatures who get epilepsy. Dogs, cats, and other animals can have seizures, too.

▸ *Grand mal* is a French term used to describe generalized seizures. It means "great sickness." Doctors now call this kind of seizure a generalized tonic-clonic seizure.

How to Learn
More about Epilepsy

At the Library: Nonfiction
Emanuele, Patricia.
Everything You Need to Know about Epilepsy.
New York: Rosen Publishing Group, 2000.

Gordon, Melanie Apel.
Let's Talk about Epilepsy.
New York: Rosen Publishing Group, 1999.

Gosselin, Kim, and Moss Freedman (Illustrator).
Taking Seizure Disorders to School: A Story about Epilepsy.
Valley Park, Mo.: JayJo Books, 1998.

O'Neill, Linda.
Having Epilepsy.
Vero Beach, Fla.: Rourke Book Company, 2001.

Pridmore, Saxby, McGrath, Mary, and Michael Chesworth (Illustrator).
Julia, Mungo, and the Earthquake: A Story for Young People about Epilepsy.
New York: Magination Press, 1991.

Schachter, Steven C., et al.
*The Brainstorms Family: Epilepsy on Our Terms: Stories by
Children with Seizures and Their Parents.*
Phildadelphia: Lippincott-Raven, 1996.

Vander Hook, Sue.
Epilepsy.
Mankato, Minn.: Smart Apple Media, 2000.

At the Library: Fiction
Moss, Deborah M.
Lee: The Rabbit with Epilepsy.
Kensington, Md.: Woodbine House, 1989.

Philbrick, Rodman.
The Last Book in the Universe.
New York: Blue Sky Press, 2000.

On the Web

Visit our home page for lots of links about epilepsy:
http://www.childsworld.com/links.html

Note to Parents, Teachers, and Librarians: We routinely verify our Web links to make sure they're safe, active sites—so encourage your readers to check them out!

Through the Mail or by Phone

The American Epilepsy Society
342 North Main Street
West Hartford, CT 06117-2507
860/586-7505

Epilepsy Education Association, Inc.
1025 Creekside Court, Apt. C
Mishawaka, IN 46544
219/273-4050

The Epilepsy Foundation
4351 Garden City Drive
Landover, MD 20785-7223
800/332-1000

The Leon Bender Foundation
2901 Piedmont Road, Suite C
Atlanta, GA 30305
770/442-7561

The Regional Epilepsy Center
325 Ninth Avenue
Box 359745
Seattle, WA 98104-2499
800/374-3627

Index

About the Author

Shirley Wimbish Gray has been a writer and educator for more than 25 years and has published more than a dozen nonfiction books for children. She also coordinates cancer education programs at the University of Arkansas for Medical Sciences and consults as a writer with scientists and physicians. She lives with her husband and two sons in Little Rock, Arkansas.